MW01291266

# HAGGADAH
# GOOD FEELING ABOUT THIS

Copyright © 2011 Michelle Slade
Illustrations by Chinthaka Herath & Shalinee Marapana
All rights reserved.
ISBN-10: 1468052217
ISBN-13: 978-1468052213

# ABOUT THIS HAGGADAH & HOW TO USE IT

## Why is this Haggadah different from all other Haggadahs?

- This Haggadah doesn't just tell us *what* to do – it also tells us *why*. Why, for example, do we need to know that five rabbis once spent all night chatting at B'nei Brak? And why on earth do we have to weigh our parsley?

- Other Haggadahs constantly go off on various tangents and they never signpost when they're doing this and why. This Haggadah keeps you in the loop from start to finish.

- Other Haggadahs are either aimed at adults or purely at children. This Haggadah will suit everyone (which means you'll all be on the same page – literally – throughout the service).

- Let's admit it: other Haggadahs manage to turn an exceptionally exciting story into a rather dreary and uninspiring one. This Haggadah livens things up a bit. (You can let me know if it's been successful in this attempt by emailing passover@michelleslade.com.)

## All other Haggadahs are in black and white. What's with all the colours on this one?

- The pictures are much more fun to look at in colour.

- The regular Passover service is the black text on the page; the explanatory text (which should help you to understand things) is on the notepad sections throughout the book.

## All other Haggadahs end with happy songs and stuff. Why does this Haggadah contain a 'References' section?

- This Haggadah takes information from a variety of sources and – for the most part – rewrites it so that it's fun and easy to understand. However, it's only polite to thank the creators of the original information.

- Sometimes this Haggadah quotes other sources verbatim. It's even more important to explicitly thank those sources (and it would be illegal to claim those particular quotes as my own).

# CONTENTS

1: Prepare a plate on the table, which contains three matzot – one on top of the other.

- The bottom one is called the *Yisrael*
- The middle one is called the *Levi*
- The top one is called the *Kohen*

*(avirtualpassover.com says that the bottom matzah is called the Binah, or Intelligence; the middle one is called the Hokhmah, or Wisdom; and the top one is called the Keter, or Crown. Other texts refer to these matzot by other different names.)*

### Why three matzot?

*The reason for three matzot differs, depending on who you ask. (As we shall soon discover, many elements of this meal represent many things depending on who you ask, so if you want to move things along, it's often best not to ask.)*

- *If you ask chabad.org, the matzot might symbolise the three castes of Jews – Israelites, Levites and Priests (also known as the Kohanes, or the Kohanim). On a practical level, three matzot are needed so that when we break the middle matzah, we are still left with the two whole ones required to pronounce the Ha-motzi – the blessing over the bread. (On Shabbat and holidays, we are supposed to say blessings over two whole loaves of bread.)*

- *If you ask chaim.org, the matzot serve as a reminder of the three Patriarchs: Abraham, Isaac and Jacob.*

- *If you ask avirtualpassover.com, the top and bottom matzot represent the double portion of manna\* that was given to the Israelites in the wilderness\*\* the day before the Sabbath. The middle matzah represents the Exodus\*\* and is the "bread of poverty", which reminds us that poor people usually break their bread and share it, or they break off a piece and put away the other piece for a later meal.*

- *One interpretation has the middle matzah representing the sacrificial lamb\*\*.*

*\*Manna is the food substance miraculously given by God to the Israelites while they wandered in the desert.*
*\*\*These all refer to the actual Passover story, which comes later.*

2: Prepare the Passover seder plate.

*This is a special plate containing symbolic foods. Each of the items arranged on the plate has special significance in the retelling of the story of the Exodus from Egypt. Below are the most common items.*

***Z'roa*** – the roasted shankbone of a lamb or goat. (Some vegetarian seders use broiled beets.)

***Maror*** – a bitter herb (most often horseradish – whole or grated).

***Chazeret*** – another bitter herb. While chazeret is not used in every Jewish community, when it does appear on the seder plate, it's usually in the form of leaves of romaine lettuce.

***Charoset*** – the sweet, brown yummy stuff. In Ashkenazi homes, charoset is traditionally made from chopped nuts, grated apples, cinnamon and sweet red wine. Sephardic recipes call for dates and honey in addition to chopped nuts, cinnamon and wine.

**Karpas** – a vegetable (other than the bitter herbs), which is dipped into salt water at the beginning of the seder service. Parsley, celery or boiled potato are usually used.

***Beitzah*** – the hard-boiled egg.

## The significance of the seder plate food

**Z'roa:** Symbolises the lamb that was offered as the special sacrifice on the eve of the Exodus from Egypt. (This was when the Israelites sacrificed a lamb and put the blood on their door posts, so that God knew to "pass over" their homes and spare their firstborn sons. There's more on this later.) In Temple times, a sacrifice was offered in the Holy Temple on the afternoon before Passover (known as the paschal* lamb). But because the Temple was destroyed**, we should no longer sacrifice a whole lamb to remember the Passover story like we used to. Until the Temple is rebuilt, we make a small gesture instead by having a bit of shankbone on a plate. The shankbone is also said to symbolise God's outstretched arm.

**Maror:** Symbolises the bitterness and harshness of the slavery endured by Jews in Egypt.

**Chazeret:** Jews are divided on the requirement of chazeret, so not all communities use it. The Haggadah recommends that we eat the paschal lamb "with unleavened bread and bitter herbs" (note the plural), and this is why most seder plates have a place for an extra bitter herb. Romaine lettuce (which has bitter-tasting roots) is recommended as the chazeret, although many people opt for radish: it adds colour.

**Charoset:** Represents the mortar*** used by the Jewish slaves when they were forced to build storehouses in Egypt. In some families, charoset is also said to remind us of the sweet taste of the promised redemption of the Hebrew people.

**Karpas:** The dipping of a simple vegetable into salt water, which represents tears, mirrors the pain felt by the Jewish slaves in Egypt.

**Beitzah:** The hard-boiled egg symbolises many different things, according to whom you ask:

• The roundness of the egg resembles the earth and life, which are constantly moving in a circle.

• Life – we are all born from an egg.

• The egg is symbolic of the festival sacrifice made in biblical times. (On Passover, an additional sacrifice was offered too – see "z'roa" above.) It is therefore a tradition of mourning, because it reminds us that since the destruction of the Temple, we cannot offer a sacrifice on festivals. It is for this reason that we don't eat the egg during the service itself (as with the z'roa) – although we can eat it as a starter before the meal. Because an

*egg represents mourning, we also eat hard-boiled eggs at funerals.*

- *It symbolises spring and the renewal brought by that season (which is the time of year that Passover is celebrated, as well).*

*\* The word "paschal" pertains to all things Passover.*
*\*\* There is more information on the destruction of the Temples later on.*
*\*\*\* Mortar is a paste used to bind construction blocks together.*

### Many Passover rituals refer to the Temple of Jerusalem; what was it? Why was it so important?

*There were actually two temples known as the Temple of Jerusalem (or "Holy Temple"): the Second Temple was rebuilt after the First Temple was destroyed – see below. They were both situated on the Temple Mount in the old city of Jerusalem.*

*Jews believe that the temples acted as a figurative "footstool" of God's presence, and that a Third Temple will be built at the same location in the future.*

*The First Temple was built by King Solomon, who reigned c.970–c.930 BCE. It was the only place of Jewish sacrifice. It was destroyed by the Bablyonians in 586 BCE, when they ruined the city.*

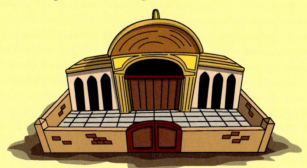

*Construction of the Second Temple began in 538 BCE and the building wasn't completed until 515 BCE. Centuries later, in around 20 BCE, the Second Temple was renovated by Herod the Great and became known as Herod's Temple. It was then destroyed by the Romans in 70 CE during the Siege of Jerusalem. Only part of the Western Wall remains standing.*

*Since the late 7th century CE, an Islamic shrine called the Dome of the Rock has stood on the site of the Second Temple. The al-Aqsa Mosque also stands in the courtyard of the old Second Temple. Temple Mount is a significant holy place in Islam too, because it has served as a sanctuary for many biblical prophets.*

**Leader:** *Pour the wine.*

**Everyone:** *Recite the Kiddush:*

בָּרוּךְ אַתָּה יְהֹוָה, אֱלֹהֵינוּ מֶלֶךְ הָעוֹלָם בּוֹרֵא פְּרִי הַגָּפֶן

Baruch attah Adonai, eloheynu melech ha-olam, boray p'ri ha-gafen.

Blessed are You, our God, King of the Universe, who creates the fruit of the vine.

בָּרוּךְ אַתָּה יי אֱלֹהֵינוּ מֶולָךְ הָעוֹלָם, שֶׁהֶחֱיָנוּ וְקִיְּמָנוּ וְהִגִּיעָנוּ לַזְּמַן הַזֶּה.

Baruch atah Adonai eloheynu melech haolam
shehechiyanu vekiyemanu vehigianu lazman hazeh.

Blessed are You, O Lord our God, King of the Universe, who has kept us alive and sustained us and permitted us to reach this season.

**Everyone:** *Drink the first cup of wine.*

***Leader**, or **Everyone**: Wash your hands.*

In some homes, a pitcher, a basin and a towel are provided to the leader of the seder, who washes his hands and in doing so, represents everyone present. At some seders, everyone washes their hands; when that's the case, two children often carry the pitcher and basin from guest to guest

### Why are we washing our hands?

*The term "delayed gratification" probably describes it best. We should be remembering what the slaves went through all those years ago, who weren't able to eat such delicious food whenever they wanted. We wash our hands to stave off the eating bit and keep ourselves hungry.*

*Other rabbis disagree (of course) about the reason: they believe we wash our hands to replicate what everyone did in the days of the Holy Temple.*

## 4 — KARPAS (DIP KARPAS IN SALT WATER AND EAT)

*Everyone:* Take the parsley or celery and dip it in salt water. This salty dish reminds us of the tears of slaves.

*Note: Each piece of parsley should be smaller than a kezayit\* (see page 8 for more information).*

*Everyone*: Recite the following blessing:

בָּרוּךְ אַתָּה יְהֹוָה אֱלֹהֵינוּ מֶלֶךְ הָעוֹלָם, בּוֹרֵא פְּרִי הָאֲדָמָה

Baruch attah Adonai, elohaynu melech ha-olam, boray p'ri ha-adamah.

Blessed are You, our God, King of the Universe, who creates the fruit of the ground.

*Everyone*: Eat.

### *What's a kezayit?

It's a Talmudic unit of volume that's about the size of an olive.

(The Talmud is a record of rabbinic discussions pertaining to Jewish law, ethics, customs and history)

Errr...I'm having a bit of trouble getting my parsley into an olive shape. It's beginning to look less parsley, more ghastly.
Yes, yes, see where you're coming from. Some rabbis have determined that a kezayit is also equal to about 25g (0.88oz). You need to eat less than a kezayit of parsley, so try to aim for 24g or less.

### Gee thanks, helpful. So now I've got to weigh my parsley??

Well, just estimate. To help you estimate the weight of your parsley, here are some things that also weigh about 24g:

- Just under five teaspoons of sugar

- About half a slice of bread

- Just over one processed cheese slice (cheddar)

- Five grapes (seedless)

### And why the kezayit rule in the first place?

You were forewarned about asking questions, but since you have, read on...

### So... why a kezayit of parsley?

A kezayit is the minimum amount of food that, when eaten, is halachically* considered "eating". This has many implications, particularly the following:

- Implications relating to what we can and can't eat as Jews, such as milk and meat: If we eat a raisin-sized piece of coq au vin immediately after drinking a double tall extra dry latte with syrup, we're all right. But if we eat a meatball the size of a pineapple, or even the size of a regular meatball (which would be a far easier simile) after drinking a peanut butter milkshake, God won't approve.

- Implications when it comes to saying the traditional prayers after all meals (i.e. not just seder meals): If we eat or drink a kezayit or more, we have to say the "after" meal prayer, which is known as "beruch achrona". (Note that we must always say the "before" meal prayer –known as beruch roshana" – before eating or drinking anything, regardless of how small the food or drink is.)

* "Halacha" relates to Jewish laws as set out in the Talmud.

### So all this weighing and measuring of the parsley, just to avoid saying a few words after eating it?

Well...we're HUNGRY! We want to eat our main meal! And we'll never get to the main meal if we keep saying prayers after eating all these bits and pieces of food along the way.

All the other funny, fiddly eating traditions (like eating the bitter herbs and matzah dipped in charoset – all coming soon) come straight before the meal – there's no gap. So we don't have to say an "after" prayer after eating each bit. But there's a MASSIVE gap between eating this parsley and eating all those other bits and pieces, so if we ate a kezayit's worth, we'd have no choice but to say the "after" prayer.

# 5 YACHATZ (BREAK THE MIDDLE MATZAH)

**Leader:** *Uncover the plate of matzah.*

**Leader:** *Take the middle matzah and break it in two, one piece larger than the other. The larger piece is set aside to serve as afikoman (which can now be hidden for children to find later). The smaller piece is put back, between the two matzot.*

### Why three pieces of matzah?

*See Chapter 1: Pre-dinner preparations.*

### Why do we break the matzah and save one (the afikoman) for later?

*The saved piece will be the final piece of food we eat at the Passover meal. (There's more on why we do this comes later – see Chapter 14: Tzafun.)*

### Why is it customary to hide this saved piece of matzavh?

*There are many explanations (of course!), but here is one: Rabbi Eliezer (an important rabbi who is mentioned in the Talmud; he crops up again later) said that one should hide the matzah so that children won't fall asleep: they'll stay awake until they're allowed by the parents to search for the afikoman.*

<table>
<tr><td>**6**</td><td># MAGGID (RECITE THE PASSOVER STORY)</td></tr>
</table>

**Leader:** *Raise the pieces of matzah.*

**Everyone:** *Say the following:*

This is the bread of affliction, which our forefathers ate in Egypt. Whoever is hungry, let him come and eat; whoever is in need, let him come and join us in celebrating the Pesach Festival. This year we are here, next year may it be in the Land of Israel. This year we are as slaves, next year as free men.

**Leader:** *Move the matzah to one side and cover it.*

*Why do we invite any Tom Rubenstein, Dick Levy or Harry Cohen into our home?*

Because we're nice! And wouldn't we feel bad if we knew that other Jews had no one to celebrate with tonight?

Also, we need to continue the traditions of our ancestors, who treated all Jews – not just blood relatives – as family. This is what helped them to overcome many barriers, and it's something that will continue to help us if we ever encounter difficulties in the future.

**Everyone:** *Pour the second cup of wine but do not drink it.*

**Everyone (or traditionally the youngest child):** *Recite the Ma Nishtana:*

מַה נִּשְׁתַּנָּה הַלַּיְלָה הַזֶּה מִכָּל הַלֵּילוֹת?

שֶׁבְּכָל הַלֵּילוֹת אָנוּ אוֹכְלִין חָמֵץ וּמַצָּה, הַלַּיְלָה הַזֶּה - כֻּלּוֹ מַצָּה.

שֶׁבְּכָל הַלֵּילוֹת אָנוּ אוֹכְלִין שְׁאָר יְרָקוֹת - הַלַּיְלָה הַזֶּה מָרוֹר.

שֶׁבְּכָל הַלֵּילוֹת אֵין אָנוּ מַטְבִּילִין אֲפִילוּ פַּעַם אֶחָת - הַלַּיְלָה הַזֶּה שְׁתֵּי פְעָמִים.

שֶׁבְּכָל הַלֵּילוֹת אָנוּ אוֹכְלִין בֵּין יוֹשְׁבִין וּבֵין מְסֻבִּין - הַלַּיְלָה הַזֶּה כֻּלָּנוּ מְסֻבִּין.

Mah nishtanah halailah hazeh,
Mikol haleilot? Mikol haleilot?

Sheb'chol haleilot, anu ochlin,
Chameits umatsah, chameits umatsah,
Halaylah hazeh, halaylah hazeh kulo matsa.
Halaylah hazeh, halaylah hazeh kulo matsa.

Sheb'chol haleilot, anu ochlin,
Sh'ar y'rakot, Sh'ar y'rakot,
Halaylah hazeh, halaylah hazeh kulo maror.
Halaylah hazeh, halaylah hazeh kulo maror.

Sheb'chol haleilot, anu matbilin,
Afilu pa'am achat, Afilu pa'am achat.
Halaylah hazeh, halaylah hazeh sh'tei p'amim,
Halaylah hazeh, halaylah hazeh sh'tei p'amim.

Sh'b'chol haleilot, anu ochlin,
Bein yoshvin uvein m'subin,

Bein yoshvin uvein m'subin,
Halaylah hazeh, halaylah hazeh, kulanu m'subin.
Halaylah hazeh, halaylah hazeh, kula ^nu m'subin.

## What makes this night different from other nights?

1.  On any other night we eat both leavened and unleavened bread; why on this night do we eat only unleavened bread?

2.  On any other night we eat herbs of all kinds; why on this night do we eat only bitter herbs?

3.  On any other night we do not dip our herbs even once; why on this night do we dip them twice?

4.  On any other night we eat our meals either sitting upright, or reclining; why on this night do we all recline?

*Leader: Put the matzah back where it was at the beginning, and partially uncover it.*

### A note on the Four Questions

The purpose of the Four Questions is to arouse curiosity in children. These Four Questions have become fixed over time, but we always hope that children will come up with their own questions too. Children generally sing the Four Questions out loud. (If you don't know the tune that is typically used to sing these questions, just type "Ma Nishtana" into YouTube.)

# MAGGID – SECOND PREAMBLE (THE ANSWER TO THE BIG FOUR QUESTIONS)

The answer to the main question ("Why is this night different from all other nights?") is this:

We were slaves to a Pharaoh in Egypt, and the Eternal led us out from there with a mighty hand and an outstretched arm. Had not the Holy One led our ancestors out of Egypt, we and our children and our children's children would still be enslaved.

So even if we're very much aware of this story through reading the Torah, it's still our duty to recite it every year.

### What about the sub-questions (matzah; horseradish; herbs; slouching)?

*These questions are considered to be part of the main "different from other nights" question. Therefore they don't get a direct answer in the Haggadah. However, Michael Rubiner's Two-Minute Haggadah succinctly provides:*

- *(About the matzah) When we left Egypt, we were in a hurry. There was no time for making decent bread.*

- *(About the horseradish) Life was bitter, like horseradish.*

- *(About the herbs) It's called symbolism.*

- *(About the slouching) Free people get to slouch.*

# 6C MAGGID – THIRD PREAMBLE (OFF-ON-A-TANGENT STORY ABOUT FIVE RABBIS)

*The rabbi dudes mentioned in the passage below recited the Passover story together many years ago (although they discussed it all night, which may be overdoing it a bit). We should follow their example by reciting the Passover story each year.*

It once happened when Rabbi Eliezer [el'ee-EE-zuhr], Rabbi Yehoshua [yuh-HOSH-yoo-uh], Rabbi Elazar [el-AY-zuhr] ben Azaryah [az'uh-RI-uh], Rabbi Akiva and Rabbi Tarphon were celebrating the seder in B'nei Brak. They were discussing the Exodus of their forefathers from Egypt the whole night until their pupils came and said to them, "Rabbis, it is time for the recital of the morning Shema."

**Why do we need to know that the rabbis were up all night discussing the story? Is it just to make sure we do it too?**

*These rabbis' names appear throughout the Talmud (a record of rabbinic discussions pertaining to Jewish law, ethics, customs and history), so they're pretty important people. And it's no surprise that they can engage in lengthy discourse on matters of Judaism. But this particular conversation was important, because while they were busy talking about their forefathers being saved by God, they were technically lying (if you account for genealogy only in the very literal sense): none of them was descended from slaves. How could these rabbis be so involved in a story that didn't directly concern them or their family?*

*But here's the thing: the Jewish people are one entity. We may have different names and live in different areas, but we're still interconnected and our fates are inextricably tied to one another. If one Jew suffers, then the rest of us are responsible for easing that suffering. Something that happens to our proverbial neighbour also concerns us. This unity of experience, and consequent unity of purpose, should drive us every day – just as it drove those rabbis. Rather than saying, "At least my family wasn't enslaved", they said "My people were enslaved; my brethren were oppressed. Let us celebrate their redemption and ours, and let us pray for God to redeem us again."*

*There's more: This story takes place during the rule of the Roman Emperor Hadrian, who (as described later) made the Israelites' lives hell and ordered the destruction of the Second Temple. These rabbis in the story were part of a resistance movement against Roman occupation, and their headquarters were at B'nei Brak – where this story of the seder takes place. The seder was used to plan a strategy of resistance against Roman occupation as well as to discuss their ancestors. So although the rabbis weren't descended from the original slaves, they were still persecuted (as Jews have been throughout history).*

This chapter has help from the *Two-Minute Haggadah* by Michael Rubiner.

בָּרוּךְ הַמָּקוֹם, בָּרוּךְ הוּא. בָּרוּךְ שֶׁנָּתַן תּוֹרָה לְעַמּוֹ יִשְׂרָאֵל, בָּרוּךְ הוּא.
כְּנֶגֶד אַרְבָּעָה בָנִים דִּבְּרָה תוֹרָה.
אֶחָד חָכָם, וְאֶחָד רָשָׁע, וְאֶחָד תָּם, וְאֶחָד שֶׁאֵינוֹ יוֹדֵעַ לִשְׁאוֹל.

Baruch haMakom. Baruch Hu. Baruch she-natan Torah l'amo yisrael.
Baruch hu.
K'neged arba'ah vanim dibrah Torah. Echad chacham, echad rasha, echad
tam, v'echad she'aino yodea lishol.

Blessed is the Place (The Almighty, who is present in all places). Blessed is
He. Blessed is He who gave the Torah to his people Israel. Blessed is He.
The Torah speaks of four different types of children. One is wise, one is
wicked, one is simple and one does not even know how to ask.

* The wise one, what does he say? "What are the testimonies, statutes and
  laws that God commanded you?"

  You are to instruct him in the Laws of Pesach and that after the Pesach
  Offering, we are not to eat anything apart from the afikoman. (In other
  words, we should explain Passover.)

* The simple one, what does he say? He says, "What does this mean?"

  To him you say, "With a strong hand, God brought us out of Egypt, out of
  the house of bondage." (In other words, we should explain Passover slowly.)

- The wicked one, what does he say? He says, "What does this service mean to you?

  He says, "to you". And because he has excluded himself from the community, he has denied the essentials of our faith. You are to answer him harshly and say, "Because of this God did for me when I came out of Egypt." You say "for me" and not "for you". Had he been there he would not have been among the redeemed. (In other words, we should browbeat him in front of the relatives.)

- And the one who does not know how to ask?

  You must speak to him as it says in the Scripture: "Because God did this for me when I went out of Egypt." (Say it loudly to embarrass him and make sure he speaks up in future.)

# MAGGID –
# THE STORY (FINALLY!)

Once upon a time, God made the following promises to Abraham and his wife Sarah in a covenant (after Abraham had proved his love and devotion to God):

• The promise of a national land

• The promise of numerous descendants

• The promise of blessings and redemption

God repeated these promises to each new generation – to Isaac and Rebecca, and to Jacob, Rachel and Leah. Presumably He had other things to tend to, which is why it took a while for Him to see through on His promises.

Then once upon a later time, someone called Joseph (he of the absurdly unfashionable technicolour coat) came to live in Egypt as an adviser to Pharaoh Elvis*. Joseph's starving hungry family then followed him from Canaan, where Pharaoh Elvis allowed them to remain. The family stayed in Egypt in peace for many generations, and became known as the Israelites.

*Contemporary reference to the Andrew Lloyd-Webber musical. (See YouTube.)

### *How did Joseph come to be Pharaoh's adviser in Egypt?*

*When Joseph lived in the land of Canaan with his family, he had dreams that correctly predicted the seven years of feast and subsequent seven years of famine that Egypt would have to endure – and he helped the Egyptians to prepare for it by telling them to store food during the feast. So Pharaoh Elvis decided that Joseph would be a useful guy to have around.*

### *Where is the land of Canaan?*

*Canaan is an ancient term for a region that extends from Lebanon southwards across Gaza to the Nile, and eastward to the Jordan River Valley – thus including modern Israel and the Palestinian Territories.*

Many years and many Pharaohs later, one particular Pharaoh came to rule who didn't know the story of Joseph (presumably the theatre had stopped showing the production). This was a Pharaoh with a very suspicious mind. He was scared that the Israelites would become too numerous and too powerful. He said to his people: "Look at how rich and powerful the Israelites are. If war comes, they may form alliances with our enemies and fight against us." But rather than asking the Israelites to love him tender, as Pharaoh Elvis might have done, this Pharaoh decided to have a little less conversation and just make them slaves instead.

Pharaoh forced the Israelites to do hard labour things like build cities with clay bricks. The Israelites couldn't sleep nor rest, and they were miserable and in pain. But the cruellest thing that Pharaoh did was this: he ordered every baby boy born to an Israelite woman to be drowned in the River Nile. One couple, Amram and Yocheved, did not want to comply with this order (understandable, really). Instead, they hid their infant son in their hut for three months. When his cries became too loud, Yocheved placed him in a basket on the river (a "Moses basket", if you will), near where the Pharaoh's daughter was known to bathe. Their daughter Miriam watched over the baby in the basket to see what would happen.

When Pharaoh's daughter came to bathe in the river, she discovered the basket and the baby, as his parents and sister had planned. She decided she would keep the beautiful baby for herself and named him Moshe (Moses), which means "drawn from the water". Miriam asked the princess if she needed a nurse to help her with the baby. The princess said yes, so Miriam

grabbed Yocheved and took her to the palace. So, Yocheved was able to care for her own son and secretly teach him about his heritage. (There isn't any information on what happens to poor old Amram, so let's hope he and Yocheved get to hook up in cheap motels every so often.)

A "Moses basket"!

Moses (whose name is mentioned only once in the Haggadah!) could have lived at Pharaoh's palace for the rest of his life, but he couldn't ignore the suffering of his people. Once, he saw an Egyptian beating an Israelite slave; he couldn't control his anger and he killed the Egyptian. Moses knew his life would be in danger when news of the killing spread, so he fled to the land of Midian and became a shepherd.

*(Midian is a geographical place mentioned in the Bible. It is also the fourth studio album of metal band Cradle of Filth.)*

On one occasion while he tended to his sheep, Moses saw a burning bush. From the bush, God's voice called out to Moses, saying: "I am the God of your ancestors. I have seen the suffering of the Israelites and have heard

their cries. I am ready to take them out of Egypt and bring them to the new land – a land flowing with milk and honey." God told Moses to return to Egypt and pass on this message to the Israelites; Moses was also told to warn Pharaoh that God would bring plagues to the Egyptians if the slaves weren't freed.

Moses returned to Egypt and asked Pharaoh to free the Israelites, but Pharaoh refused. So God brought ten plagues on the Egyptians.

## The complete story of the plagues (which aren't mentioned in so much detail in the Haggadah)

*Plague after plague descended upon the Egyptians. At first these calamities seemed like natural disasters, but it soon became clear that something more sinister was afoot...*

1. *The Nile's water turned to blood, which meant that all the fish died and made Egypt smell rather horrible. But Pharaoh was sceptical that this was the hand of God at work (he considered himself to be quite good at casting spells himself), so he didn't think much of it.*

2. *Hordes of frogs overran Egypt. Pharaoh was a bit more worried about this one, and he promised Moses that he'd let the Israelites leave if God*

*removed all the frogs. So God removed all the frogs. This pretty much proved that God was behind the plagues, but Pharaoh didn't admit it and went back on his promise: the Israelites were forced to stay.*

3. *The third plague was lice. The Egyptian sorcerers were itching to replicate this plague (eh, eh?!) but just could nit do it.*

4. *A grievous swarm of flies came to Egypt. These were no ordinary flies: they were killer flies, beastly flies, and they caused immense harm to people and livestock.*

*It should be mentioned at this stage that these plagues didn't affect the Israelites, who stayed as happy and as healthy as any oppressed, starving and overworked-yet-plagueless slaves might.*

5. *An epidemic disease exterminated Egyptian livestock. Once again, the Israelites' cattle were unharmed. But, as usual, Pharaoh refused to say in public what he knew in his head: with this pestilence, God was punishing him and the other Egyptians. He still refused to let the Israelites go. Surely it was just a matter of time before he'd give in, though, so God carried on...*

6. *The Egyptian people erupted in boils.*

7. *The seventh plague was a catastrophic hailstorm, which heavily damaged Egyptian orchards and crops, as well as more people and livestock.*

8. *Next there were locusts, which settled on the land and ate whatever was growing. This was great for the Egyptian kids who hated cabbage and broccoli, but not so brilliant for the health nuts who were keen on getting their "five a day".*

*Pharaoh's advisers now knew for certain that something terrible was happening to them, because all these natural disasters were certainly no coincidence. They pleaded with Pharaoh to send the Israelites away.*

*But Pharaoh was an obstinate man, oh a very obstinate man. "I am the ruler of Egypt," he proclaimed. "Egypt is the most powerful and highly revered country in the world – just look at how many people come to Sharm el-Sheikh on holiday each year. And I am the most powerful man in the world. I'm also the best looking and best dressed. Who else has a linen robe that so beautifully*

*shows off his biceps? Who else, who else I ask you, can put on eyeliner so neatly? How dare this alien God come and tell me what to do!"*

9. *A plague of darkness affected Egypt next. Before anyone had a chance to go and buy carrots and environmentally friendly light bulbs, the darkness became so thick that they couldn't see. No one could work or even socialise, and the markets all closed.*

*By now, the regular Egyptians had realised that something was up, and they thought it might have something to do with the Israelites. They begged Pharaoh to send the Israelites away, but Pharaoh was, as we know, an obstinate man, oh a very obstinate man.*

*Well, perhaps he wasn't that obstinate, because he then relented a bit and said that the Israelites could leave Egypt and go into the desert to worship their God if the plagues stopped – although they couldn't take their animals with them. But Moses said no: "We all go – our men, our women, our children, our flocks and our herds."*

*Moses's bravura didn't quite have the desired effect, because Pharaoh once again refused to let any of the Israelites go. So then God dealt his final blow:*

10. *THE BIG ONE, THE MIGHTY ONE, THE PLAGUE AGAINST WHICH ALL FUTURE PLAGUES SHALL BE BENCHMARKED: death of the firstborn. As The Man Himself (God) said: "About midnight I will go throughout Egypt. Every firstborn son in Egypt will die, from the firstborn son of Pharaoh, who sits on the throne, to the firstborn son of the slave girl, who is at her hand mill, and all the firstborn of the cattle as well. There will be loud wailing throughout Egypt – worse than there has ever been or ever will be again."*

*Before the plague, God had commanded Moses to inform all the Israelites to sacrifice a lamb and mark the doorposts of their houses with the lamb's blood. God would then know to pass over these houses and spare the lives of the Israelite firstborns.*

*Pharaoh was thoroughly annoyed after this one, and he told Moses and his people to take a hike. Moses thought, "Result!" The Israelites didn't hesitate, and that night they were led by Moses out of Egypt "with arms upraised". They left Egypt so quickly that there was no time to allow their packed lunch of not-yet-baked bread dough. So they had to eat their falafel-and-hummus sandwiches on flat, cracker-like bread – not great, but better than the inedible cardboard they had been made to eat as slaves. And anyway, they were free – YAAAAAY!*

# Back to the Haggadah...

The Lord took us out of Egypt with a strong hand and an outstretched arm, and with a great manifestation, and with signs and wonders. The Lord took us out of Egypt, not through an angel, not through a seraph and not through a messenger. The Holy One, blessed be He, did it in His glory by Himself!

*Everyone:* *You know that cup of wine you poured ages ago? You can't drink it. Instead, you've got to spill one drop of wine for each of the ten plagues:*

| | |
|---|---|
| Blood | דָּם |
| Frogs | צְפַרְדֵּעַ |
| Lice | כִּנִּים |
| Insects | עָרוֹב |
| Cattle disease | דֶּבֶר |
| Boils | שְׁחִין |
| Hail | בָּרָד |
| Locusts | אַרְבֶּה |
| Darkness | חֹשֶׁךְ |
| Slaying of the first born | מַכַּת בְּכוֹרוֹת |

DOM. TZ'FAR-DAY-A. KI-NEEM. O-ROV. DE-VER. SH'CHEEN. BO'ROD. ARBEH. CHO-SHECH. MA-KAS B'CHO-ROS.

Blood. Frogs. Lice. Insects (flies). Cattle disease. Boils. Hail. Locusts. Darkness. Slaying of the first born.

*Everyone:* *Refill your cup of wine.*

*Why were the plagues necessary? Surely God can perform miracles and could have just made the Egyptians send away their slaves without all this bother?*

*You would have thought, wouldn't you? But in fact there are two very convincing explanations for why God didn't do it this way:*

1. *If the Israelites had just got up and left, it would seem that they had been able to do everything themselves. The prospective Jewish nation wouldn't believe that it was God's doing that they were released from bondage, and instead would think that they'd achieved freedom through their own power and cleverness. That would lead the Jews to be arrogant and smug, and God wouldn't get any credit for being amazing.*

2. *The Egyptians would have got off scot-free for oppressing the Israelites, which would have been unfair and made for a rather boring Haggadah story.*

As we know, Pharaoh was an obstinate man, oh a very obstinate man. He was also, as we have seen, an indecisive man, oh a very indecisive man. (Or was he? He's not sure.) And this indecisiveness was to continue: as soon as he let the Israelites leave Egypt, he changed his freakin' mind and ordered his soldiers to bring them back. The soldiers caught up with the Israelites by the banks of the Red Sea, causing the Israelites to gasp and cry in horror – for let's not forget that these soldiers were fish-smelling, lice-infested, boil-covered and badly dressed soldiers (on account of putting their clothes on in the dark). The Israelites may have also gasped and cried because they were desperate to flee Egypt and reach freedom.

But God saved the day again: he told Moses to lift his rod, and when he did, a strong wind drove back the sea – leaving space for the Israelites to cross on dry land to Canaan. The Egyptians came after them into the sea, but Moses again lifted his rod and the waters rushed back, covering the Egyptians and their horses.

Now let's remind ourselves why God was so brilliant:

**Five stanzas of leaving slavery**

1.  If He had brought us out of Egypt, it would have been enough, dayenu.

2.  If He had executed justice upon the Egyptians, it would have been enough, dayenu.

3.  If He had executed justice upon their gods, it would have been enough, dayenu.

4.  If He had slain their firstborn, it would have been enough, dayenu.

5.  If He had given to us their health and wealth, it would have been enough, dayenu.

## Five stanzas of miracles

6. If He had split the sea for us, it would have been enough, dayenu.

7. If He had led us through on dry land, it would have been enough, dayenu.

8. If He had drowned our oppressors, it would have been enough, dayenu.

9. If He had provided for our needs in the wilderness for 40 years, it would have been enough, dayenu.*

10. If He had fed us manna, it would have been enough, dayenu.

## Five stanzas of being with God

11. If He had given us Shabbat, it would have been enough, dayenu.

12. If He had led us to Mount Sinai, it would have been enough, dayenu.

13. If He had given us the Torah, it would have been enough, dayenu.

14. If He had brought us into the land of Israel, it would have been enough, dayenu.

15. If He had built the Temple for us, it would have been enough, dayenu.

*During Line 9 ("If He had provided for our needs..."), Jews who celebrate their seders in Afghanistan and Iran hit each other over the head with green onions. It is thought that by beating each other with the onions, they remind themselves not to yearn for Egypt or to forget Egyptian bondage.

**Everyone:** *Sing the Dayenu song.*

### Please explain these 15 stanzas of leaving slavery/miracles/being with God (if it can be explained quickly)

This section tells us about what happened to the Israelites once they'd crossed the Red Sea. They wandered around the desert for forty years, eating a very restrictive diet of manna to sustain them. (Manna was a miraculous food substance that produced no "waste" – meaning the Israelites didn't need to worry about where to "go".) They were also given the gift of the Sabbath – the one day in every seven in which they could forget about their worldly problems and devote their time to family and to God.

They then reached Mount Sinai*, where Moses received the Torah (which included the Ten Commandments) from God. Finally they reached the land of Israel, where God provided them with their own Temple. This Temple was later to be destroyed twice (see Chapter 1: Pre-dinner preparation) and has not been rebuilt since.

*There are many conflicting theories on where Mount Sinai is/was located. It's generally agreed that it was a mythical mountain.

### "Dayenu" (meaning "It would have been enough"): isn't it a bit wrong to say that we didn't need Him to give us the Torah or the land of Israel? Are we saying He shouldn't have bothered?

We're a chirpy lot, us Jews – very much glass half-full. We look around the world, nod with satisfaction and think to ourselves, "Yep, I'm happy. This is enough. And you know what? I'd be happy even if we'd stopped at the achievement before this one." We're still super grateful for all that God has done for us though.

## 6F MAGGID – "ENDAMBLE" (A THIRD OFF-ON-A-TANGENT STORY – ABOUT THE SIGNIFICANCE OF THE FOOD)

Rabban Gamaliel* (see page 33) used to say "Whosoever does not speak of these three things on Pesach has not fulfilled his obligation, and they are the Pesach offering (the sacrificial lamb), matzah and maror." So now we must talk about and explain these three things in turn.

**Person reading:** *Point to the piece of roasted meat (representing the Passover offering).*

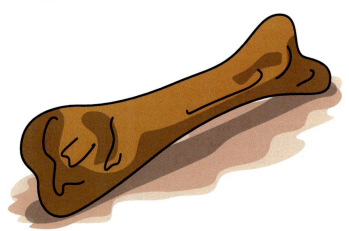

The Pesach offering that our forefathers ate in the Temple, when the Temple was standing, what was the reason for it? Because the Holy One, Blessed be He, passed over the houses of our ancestors in Egypt. As it says, "You shall say it is the Pesach offering for the Lord who 'passed over' the houses of the children of Israel in Egypt when He struck at Egypt and saved our houses..."

*Ohhhh, so THAT'S why it's called Passover! Duh!*

### About the pesach offering (see page 32)

*The z'roa on the seder plate – the roasted meat – represents the sacrificial lamb from the Passover story, which helped to save the Israelites' lives. But (and this bit is also explained in Chapter 1: Pre-dinner preparations), because the Temple was destroyed, we should no longer sacrifice a whole lamb to remember the Passover story like we used to, when the Temple was still around. Until the Temple is rebuilt, we make a small gesture instead by having a bit of shankbone on a plate.*

**Person reading:** *Lift up the matzah.*

The matzah that we eat, why do we eat it? Because the dough of our ancestors (at the time of the Exodus) did not have time to rise, when the King of Kings, the Holy One Blessed Be He, redeemed them (took them out of Egypt). As it says, "And they baked the dough which they took out of Egypt as Matzot and not leavened, because they were driven out of Egypt and they could not delay their leaving and prepare provisions."

**Person reading:** *Lift up the maror.*

This maror that we eat, for what reason do we eat it? Because the Egyptians made the lives of our ancestors in Egypt bitter. As it says, "And their lives were made bitter with hard labour, with mortar and bricks and all kinds of work in the field, with all the backbreaking work they [the Egyptians] made them do with rigour."

**Person reading:** *Put down the maror.*

### *Who the heck was Rabban Gamaliel? Four questions about him:

*So who was he? What did he do? And what's the difference between a rabban and a rabbi? And why does this man's opinion matter so much that he gets a whole bit of Haggadah to himself? No more will you have to concern yourself with these questions, for Wikipedia (among other sources) has provided the answers...*

### Who was Rabban Gamaliel?

He was the first post-temple[1] nasi[2] of the Sanhedrin[3] (explanations are a lot harder when each darn word needs an explanation all of its own). He ruled with a strong hand.

[1] After the Second Temple – the centre of Jewish worship – had been destroyed by the Romans
[2] President
[3] The supreme legislative body of the time

### What did he do?

One of his most significant achievements was the establishment of the text of the Amidah – the central prayer recited three times a day. (That's the one that sounds fun when you say it in Hebrew: A-do-nai s'fa-tai tif-tach...) This answer pretty much answers the fourth question ("Why does his opinion matter so much that he gets a whole bit of Haggadah to himself?"): it's because he wrote a very long prayer with a fun first line.

Another couple of things about Rabban Gamaliel, which aren't mentioned much in Jewish history books: He excommunicated his own brother-in-law, and he had a big fight with someone about calendar fixing (the precursor to insider trading...sort of), which humiliated another rabban in the process. This led to a rabbinic revolt against Gamaliel's leadership of the Sanhedrin. (This trivia will come in useful if anyone tells you that Gamaliel's THE MAN.)

### What's the difference between a rabban and a rabbi?

In the era after the destruction of the Second Temple, sages who were presidents of the Sanhedrin were called rabban, while all other sages at the time were called rabbis. And that seems to be about it.

# IN EVERY GENERATION...
# (REFLECTING ON THE STORY)

In every generation a person is obligated to regard himself as if he had come out of Egypt, as it is said: "You shall tell your child on that day, it is because of this that the Lord did for me when I left Egypt."

God did not just redeem our forefathers, but us, too: "And us He brought out of there [Egypt] so that He could bring us to the land which He swore to our forefathers, to give us."

**Leader:** *Cover the matzah completely.*

**Everyone:** *Raise your cup of wine (we're still on the second cup here).*

*Read the next few sections in turn as normal.*

Thus it is our duty to thank, to laud, to praise, to glorify, to exalt, to adore, to bless, to elevate and to honor the One who did all these miracles for our fathers and for us. He took us from slavery to freedom, from sorrow to joy, and from mourning to festivity, and from deep darkness to great light and from bondage to redemption. Let us therefore recite before Him Halle-luyah, Praise God!

**Everyone:** *Keep holding that wine.*

Halleluyah – praise God! Offer praise, you servants of the Lord; praise the Name of the Lord. May the Lord's Name be blessed from now and to all eternity. From the rising of the sun to its setting, the Lord's Name is praised. The Lord is high above all nations, His glory is over the heavens. Who is like the Lord, our God, who dwells on high yet looks down so low upon heaven and earth! He raises the poor from the dust, He lifts the needy from the dunghill, to seat them with nobles, with the nobles of His people. He restores the barren woman to the house, into a joyful mother of children. Halleluyah – praise God.

***Everyone:*** *Keep holding that wine.*

Blessed are You, God, our God, King of the universe, who has redeemed us and redeemed our fathers from Egypt, and enabled us to attain this night to eat matzah and maror. So too, God, our God and God of our fathers, enable us to attain other holidays and festivals that will come to us in peace with happiness in the rebuilding of Your city, and with rejoicing in Your service (in the Temple of Jerusalem). Then we shall eat the sacrifices and of the Pesach offerings, whose blood shall be sprinkled on the wall of Your altar for acceptance; and we shall thank You with a new song for our redemption and for the deliverance of our souls. Blessed are You, God, who redeemed Israel.

***Everyone:*** *Keep holding that wine and recite the following blessing:*

בָּרוּךְ אַתָּה יְהוָה, אֱלֹהֵינוּ מֶלֶךְ הָעוֹלָם בּוֹרֵא פְּרִי הַגָּפֶן

Baruch attah Adonai, eloheynu melech ha-olam, boray p'ri ha-gafen.

Blessed are You, Lord our God, King of the universe, who creates the fruit of the vine.

***Everyone:*** *Oy vey, what an achy arm! You can drink the wine now!*

# RACHTZAH (WASH HANDS, TAKE 2 – WE SAY THE BLESSING THIS TIME)

*Everyone:* Wash hands and say:

בָּרוּךְ אַתָּה יְיָ אֱלֹהֵ,ינוּ מֶ,לֶךְ הָעוֹלָם אֲשֶׁר קִדְּשָׁ,נוּ בְּמִצְוֹתָיו וְצִנָּ,נוּ עַל נְטִילַת יָדַ,יִם.

Baruch ata adonay eloheinu melech ha'olam
asher kidshanu bemitzvotav ve-tzivanu al netilat yadayim.

Bless you, Lord our God, Ruler of the universe,
Who made us holy with Your commandments, and bade us wash our hands.

*Everyone:* Don't speak until after making the next two blessings (motzi and matzah) and eating the matzah.

## 9 MOTZI (BLESS THE BREAD)

**Leader:** *Hold all three pieces of matzah.*

**Everyone:** *Say:*

בָּרוּךְ אַתָּה יְיָ אֱלֹהֵ,ינוּ מֶ,לֶךְ הָעוֹלָם הַמּוֹצִיא לֶ,חֶם מִן הָאָרֶץ.

Baruch ata adonay eloheinu melech ha'olam
ha'motzi lechem min ha'aretz.

Bless you, Lord our God, Ruler of the universe,
Who brings forth bread from the earth.

## 10 MATZAH (BLESS – AGAIN – ONE OF THE PIECES OF BREAD, AND EAT)

**Leader:** *Do not break anything off the matzot. First put down the third matzah (the bottom one).*

**Everyone:** *Recite the following blessing over the middle (broken) matzah and the top one:*

בָּרוּךְ אַתָּה יְיָ אֱלֹהֵ‎ֽ‎ינוּ מֶ‎ֽ‎לֶךְ הָעוֹלָם אֲשֶׁר קִדְּשָׁ‎ֽ‎נוּ בְּמִצְוֹתָיו וְצִוָּ‎ֽ‎נוּ עַל אֲכִילַת מַצָּה.

Baruch ata adonay eloheinu melech ha'olam
asher kidshanu bemitzvotav
ve'tzivanu al achilat matzah.

Bless you, Lord our God, Ruler of the universe,
Who made us holy with Your commandments, and bade us eat unleavened bread.

**Leader:** *Break off a kezayit of the two pieces held (we all know how much that is now), and eat the two pieces together in a reclining position. Pass the matzot around for everyone to do the same.*

## 11 MAROR (BLESS THE BITTER HERBS, AND EAT)

**Everyone:** *Dip the bitter herbs (at least a kezayit's worth) in charoset and say:*

בָּרוּךְ אַתָּה יְיָ אֱלֹהֵ ֫ ינוּ מֶ ֫ לֶךְ הָעוֹלָם אֲשֶׁר קִדְּשָׁ ֫ נוּ בְּמִצְוֹתָיו וְצִנָּ ֫ נוּ עַל אֲכִילַת מָרוֹר.

Baruch ata adonay eloheinu melech ha'olam
asher kidshanu bemitzvotav ve'tzivanu al achilat maror.

Bless you, Lord our God, Ruler of the universe,
Who made us holy with Your commandments, and bade us eat the bitter herb.

**Everyone:** *Eat the bitter herbs dipped in charoset.*

### Why do we eat the maror dipped in charoset?

The maror represents the bitterness of bondage and the charoset symbolises the mortar for the bricks our ancestors laid in Egypt. (See Chapter 1: Pre-dinner preparations, for more on this.) But charoset is also sweet. According to one interpretation, this is apparently to remind us that some-times enslavement can be "masked in familiar sweetness"; this may be stretching the metaphor a bit. Eating the two together, we remind ourselves to seek a balance between sweetness and bitterness in life.

# KOREICH
# (MMMM, SANDWICHES)

**Leader:** *Make a sandwich out of two pieces of the bottom matzah and a kezayit (oh yeseree) of maror. Pass the matzot and maror around for everyone else to do the same. Don't eat them yet.*

On Passover, in the days of the Temple in Jerusalem, Rabbi Hillel would eat a sandwich made of the Pesach lamb offering, matzah and maror. Now we do not bring sacrifices to the Temple [as discussed in Chapter 6f: Maggid – endamble], so our sandwich is made only with matzah and maror.

**Everyone:** *Now eat them together – in the reclining position.*

### Why do we eat a sandwich made of matzah and maror?

*According to one interpretation, we are combining the bread of liberation with a remembrance of the bitterness of slavery. We are creating a "physical representation of the holiday's central dialectical tension" (so says The Velveteen Rabbi's Haggadah for Passover).*

# SHULCHAN OREICH (FOOOOOOD)

**Everyone:** *You won't believe this: you can eat!!!*

*And you're allowed to get wasted, according to the Haggadah: "Now eat and drink to your need. It is permitted to drink wine between the second and third cups."*

*(The second cup was drunk before the meal; the third cup comes after the meal.)*

*Kids can search for the afikoman while waiting for the food to be served (or after they've eaten).The tradition goes that an adult will hide the afikoman somewhere in the home, and all the children must try to find it. The adult then tries to "buy" the afikoman back from the child who found it (with chocolate, money, etc.).*

### Some jokes while you wait for the food to hit your plate:

• *Why do we have a Haggadah at Passover? So we can seder right words.*

• *What do you call someone who derives pleasure from the bread of affliction? A matzochist.*

• *What kind of cheese do you eat on Passover? Matzo-rella.*

# TZAFUN
# (EAT THE AFIKOMAN)

**Everyone:** *After the meal and dessert, take the afikoman and divide it among all the members of the household. Eat it in a reclining position. If there isn't enough to go around, you can add more pieces of matzah to each person's portion. Everyone must have a kezayit's worth of afikoman, to fulfil the mitzvah of eating afikoman. (As we know, anything less than a kezayit doesn't count as food; see Chapter 4: Karpas).*

*Eat the afikoman before midnight, and don't eat anything else for the rest of the evening afterwards. (You're allowed to drink the last two cups of wine – we'll get to these in a bit – and tea, coffee or water.)*

### What is the significance of eating this matzah at the end of the meal?

*"Afikoman" means "that which comes after" or "dessert". It serves as a substitute for the paschal lamb\*, which was the last thing eaten at the Passover meal during the eras of the First and Second Temples and during the period of the Mishkan (the portable place of worship used by the Israelites while they were wandering around the desert for 40 years).*

*The Talmud says that it is forbidden to eat any other food after eating the afikoman, in order to keep the taste of matzah in our mouths. As usual, there are many explanations for why that's important. An overall summary of the reasons is that it's to remember – to remember the suffering of the Israelites; to remember the paschal lamb (see above); to remember to say Hallel (a collection of joyous Psalms).*

*We have to eat the afikoman before midnight because during the days of the Temple the paschal lamb was also eaten before midnight. (Would we jump off a cliff if all the rabbis jumped off a cliff in the days of the Temple? Would we? Would we?)*

*\*See Chapter 1: Pre-dinner preparations – particularly the bit about "z'roa" for more information on the paschal lamb, and also for more information on the First and Second Temples.*

# BEREICH (GRACE AFTER MEALS) – PREAMBLE

***Everyone:*** *Pour a third cup of wine.*

> *Bereich may start with a zimmun:*
> *If three or more people over the age of Bar Mitzvah are present (a quorum called a "mezuman"), one of them has to invite everyone to take part in the grace after meals – called Birkat Hamazon. The invitation is called a "zimmun" – see below.*
>
> *It is preferable if a minyan (ten or more people) is present. The minyan must say the bracketed words below as well. This invitation is called a "zimmun b'shem". In Orthodox Judaism, the three (or ten) people must be male. (For more information on this, see the section below called "Women zwimmen".)*
>
> *If there aren't three males present, then just launch straight into the main section below that begins, "Blessed are You, Lord, our God..."; then cackle with glee that you're able to save time and get to bed a bit earlier.*

## Zimmun (the invitation)

***Leader:*** Let us say Grace.

***Everyone:*** May the Name of the Lord be blessed now and for ever.

***Leader:*** Let us bless the One [our God], whose food we have eaten.

***Everyone:*** Let us bless the One [our God], whose food we have eaten and through whose goodness we live.

> ### What is the reason for preferring a minyan for prayers?
>
> *There's an awful lot written on this, but the main gist is as follows: it is a firm belief that wherever ten Israelites are assembled – either for worship or for the study of the law – the Divine Presence dwells among them. (Those who meet for prayer or study in smaller groups are also to be praised, but there is a special merit and sacredness to the minyan of ten.)*

*This is why we say "Our God" in the prayers only if ten people are praying: it is when God dwells among the people praying.*

*Some scholars believe that an individual is obligated to seek a minyan of ten before praying; others stress that people should only pray in this way together if they all happen to be around at the same time.*

### And what about a mezuman? When is it okay to just have three people available for prayers?

*Ten people is definitely preferable, but if ten people aren't around, another significant threshold is three people. Three people is enough to create a holy community necessary for prayer.*

*It's still okay to pray alone, but a minimum of three people – or preferably ten – is best.*

### Women zwimmen (or zimmun, to be more precise)

*The Talmud states that women are obligated to say Birkat Hamazon and therefore three women can form the mezuman and lead a zimmun. But later authorities held that women were exempt from leading a zimmun. A number of modern Orthodox authorities state that women can (indeed some say they should) form a mezuman.*

*A minority of modern Orthodox authorities also say that ten women can (or should) constitute a minyan for purposes of saying the zimmun for Birkat Hamazon. But these Orthodox authorities (unlike Reform Jews) say that a minyan cannot be formed from a combination of men and women.*

*Capiche?*

## Mayim acharonim

*FYI: It is customary in many Orthodox communities to wash the hands before reciting Birkat Hamazon. The custom is called "mayim acharonim" (wash afterwards). A special dispenser (also called a mayim acharonim) can be used to dispense water.*

*Now say the traditional Grace After Meals (Birkat Hamazon).*
*(With thanks to the* Red Sea Haggadah.*)*

**Leader:** *Bless the Lord, blessed be His Name.*

**Everyone:**

**Blessing 1:** Blessed are You, Lord, our God, King of the universe, who, in His goodness, feeds the whole world with grace, with kindness and with mercy. He gives food to all flesh, for His kindness is everlasting. Through His great goodness to us continuously we do not lack food, and may we never lack it, for the sake of His great Name. For He is a [benevolent] God who feeds and sustains all, does good to all, and prepares food for all His creatures whom He has created, as it is said: You open Your hand and satisfy the desire of every living thing. Blessed are You Lord, who provides food for all.

*(Basically: Thanks for the food.)*

**Blessing 2:** We thank You, Lord, our God, for having given as a heritage to our fathers a precious, good and spacious land; for having brought us out, Lord our God, from the land of Egypt and redeemed us from the house of slaves; for Your covenant which You have sealed in our flesh; for Your Torah which You have taught us; for Your statutes which You have made known to us; for the life, favor and kindness which You have graciously bestowed upon us; and for the food we eat with which You constantly feed and sustain us every day, at all times, and at every hour.

*(Basically: Thanks for liberating us from Egyptian bondage and thanks for the covenant – the one with Abraham that was repeated to his descendants, which promised us the land of Israel and that requires us to circumcise all males as our side of the bargain. It's a weird deal, but we're*

*willing to go with it. Thanks also for providing us with the Torah and the commandments. And thank You for the food again.)*

### Why do we say thanks for the food twice?

*The first "thanks" is in gratitude for the manna – the "bread from heaven" mentioned earlier. The second "thanks" was introduced when the Jews entered their homeland and began to eat its produce, grown from the earth. So whether a person's bread comes easily – as the manna from heaven – or with hard work, he must thank God for it. Even the bread made as a result of hard work is from God really: it is God who makes the grain grow in the fields and enables us to harvest it.*

For all this, Lord our God, we thank You and bless You. May Your Name be blessed by the mouth of every living being, constantly and forever. As it is written: When you have eaten and are satiated, you shall bless the Lord your God, for the good land which He has given you. Blessed are You, Lord, for the land and for the food.

*(Basically: The reason we're saying thank you, by the way, is that it says in Deuteronomy that we should thank you for the land when we've had enough food to eat.)*

**Blessing 3:** Have mercy, Lord our God, upon Israel Your people, upon Jerusalem Your city, upon Zion the abode of Your Glory, upon the kingship of the house of David Your anointed, and upon the great and holy House which is called by Your Name. Our God, our Father, our Shepherd, feed us, sustain us, nourish us and give us comfort; and speedily, Lord our God, grant us relief from all our afflictions. Lord, our God, please do not make us dependent upon the gifts of mortal men nor upon their loans, but only upon Your full, open, holy and generous hand, that we may not be shamed or disgraced forever and ever.

And rebuild Jerusalem the holy city speedily in our days. Blessed are You, Lord, who in His mercy rebuilds Jerusalem. Amen.

*(Basically: Please feed us, look after us and comfort us. Don't make us depend on other people for this – we want You to do it. We hope that Israel and Jerusalem prosper and that the Temple in Jerusalem is rebuilt.)*

**Blessing 4 (Rabban Gamaliel's contribution):** Blessed are You, Lord, our God, King of the universe, benevolent God, our Father, our King, our Might, our Creator, our Redeemer, our Maker, our Holy One, the Holy One of Jacob, our Shepherd, the Shepherd of Israel, the King who is good and does good to all, each and every day. He has done good for us, He does good for us, and He will do good for us; He has bestowed, He bestows, and He will forever bestow upon us grace, kindness and mercy, relief, salvation and success, blessing and help, consolation, sustenance and nourishment, compassion, life, peace and all goodness; and may He never cause us to lack any good.

*(Basically: Way to go, God: you've done well. And thank you – you're a good guy)*

May the Merciful One reign over us forever and ever.
May the Merciful One be blessed in heaven and on earth.
May the Merciful One be praised for all generations, and be glorified in us forever and all eternity, and honoured in us forever and ever.
May the Merciful One sustain us with honour.
May the Merciful One break the yoke of exile from our neck and may He lead us upright to our land.

May the Merciful One send abundant blessing into this house and upon this table at which we have eaten.

May the Merciful One send us Elijah the Prophet, may he (Elijah) be remembered for good and may he bring us good tidings, salvation and consolation.

May the Merciful One bless my father, my teacher, the master of this house, and my mother, my teacher, the mistress of this house; them, their household, their children, and all that is theirs; us, and all that is ours. Just as He blessed our ancestors, Abraham, Isaac and Jacob, Sarah, Rebecca, Rachel and Leah "in everything", "from everything", with "everything", so may He bless all of us (the children of the Covenant) together with a perfect blessing, and let us say, Amen.

**What's with all these mini prayers tacked on to the end of Blessing 4?**

*These short prayers were added to the fourth blessing at a later date; they all ask for God's compassion.*

*A few more prayers to add on to the end:*

May we receive blessing from the Lord and just kindness from the God of our salvation, and may we find grace and good understanding in the eyes of God and man.

May the Merciful One cause us to inherit that day which is all good.

May the Merciful One grant us the privilege of reaching the days of the Messiah and the life of the World to Come. He is a tower of salvation to His King, and bestows kindness upon His anointed, to David and his descendants forever. He who makes peace in His heights, may He make peace for us and for all Israel; and say, Amen.

Fear the Lord, you His holy ones, for those who fear Him suffer no want. Young lions are in need and go hungry, but those who seek the Lord shall not lack any good. Give thanks to the Lord for He is good, for His kindness is everlasting. You open Your hand and satisfy the desire of every living thing. Blessed is the man who trusts in the Lord, and the Lord will be his trust.

**Everyone:** *Recite the blessing for the wine.*

בָּרוּךְ אַתָּה יְהֹוָה, אֱלֹהֵינוּ מֶלֶךְ הָעוֹלָם בּוֹרֵא פְּרִי הַגָּפֶן:

Baruch attah Adonai, eloheynu melech ha-olam, boray p'ri ha-gafen.

Blessed are You, Lord, our God, King of the universe, who creates the fruit of the vine.

**Everyone:** *Remember that third cup of wine you poured, ooh about three hours ago? You can drink it now – while reclining.*

### What exactly is Birkat Hamazon?

It is a set of Hebrew blessings that Jewish law prescribes following a meal. You only say it after a meal that includes bread made from any of the five principal species of grains of Israel (wheat, barley, spelt, oats and rye).

Earlier we read about eating less than a kezayit of parsley to avoid saying the "after" prayer (see Chapter 4: Karpas); this would have been a different "after" prayer from Birkat Hamazon – there are different prayers for different meals/types of food. The following website shows the "before" and "after" prayers for all different types of food: www.jewishvirtuallibrary.org/jsource/Judaism/Brachot.html.

Though technically a series of blessings, Birkat Hamazon takes the form of prayers which are typically read silently for ordinary meals, and often sung or chanted for special meals like Shabbat, religious festivals and special occasions.

### Why do we say it?

In Deuteronomy, it says: "When you have eaten and are satisfied, you shall bless the Lord your God for the good land which He gave you."

Or, as askmoses.com explains (the best explanation you'll ever read):

If you do lunch at Frank's, you'll thank Frank when you leave: you'll say, "Thanks, Frank!" If you do lunch at Frank's and the food was fantastic, you'll say, "Thanks, Frank—the food was fantastic!" And if you do lunch at Frank's and the food was fantastic and the fried fish was fabulous, you'll say, "Thanks, Frank—the food was fantastic and your fried fish was fabulous!" Bottom line is, the more you enjoy it, the more details you add. And that's why Birkat Hamazon is not a one-liner—there's a lot to thank God for.

### What's the structure of Birkat Hamazon?

It's made up of four blessings:

1. A blessing of thanks for the food, which was apparently composed by Moses in gratitude for the manna (miraculous food substance) that the Jews ate in the wilderness during the Exodus from Egypt.

2. A blessing of thanks for the land of Israel, which is attributed to Joshua after he led the Jewish people into Israel.

3. A blessing that concerns Jerusalem, which is ascribed to David (who established the capital of Jerusalem) and Solomon (who built the Temple of Jerusalem).

These three blessings are regarded as required by scriptural law.

4. A blessing of thanks for God's goodness, which was written by Rabban Gamaliel (yep, him again – see Chapter 6f: Endamble).

There is no real obligation to recite this particular blessing. Take that, Gamaliel!

Birkat Hamazon was introduced after the destruction of Betar (a Jewish fortress in Jerusalem) by Hadrian and his fellow Romans in the second century A.D. (The destruction of Betar happened on Tisha B'Av – the day that Jews commemorate the fall of the First and Second Temples. It's kind of like holding a remembrance service for your rabbit a year after its death, only for a fox to come into the garden and kill your other bunny...but much worse.)

Hadrian prevented the fallen heroes of Betar from being buried, but when Hadrian died, permission was given to bury them. Miraculously, the bodies didn't smell too bad after all those years. To commemorate the event, and to remind us that God is good, this blessing was added to Birkat Hamazon.

After these four blessings are a series of short prayers that ask for God's compassion. Additional sections are also added for special occasions.

There are several known texts for Birkhat Hamazon: Ashkenazi, Sephardic, Yemenite and Italian versions. All follow the same structure outlined above, but the wording varies.

### Do we always say the blessing over the cup of wine? Or do we only do it at Passover?

It's not obligatory, but it's customary for the person leading the zimmun (see Chapter 15: Bereich preamble) to recite the blessings over a cup of wine (called the kos shel baracha – cup of blessing). At Passover, the cup of blessing is drunk by everyone present; it's also the third cup.

We have eaten the feast of our freedom and we have recalled the redemption of our people. But the dream of Passover transcends the Jew and reaches out to all people.

Many centuries ago, there lived a prophet whose name was Elijah. He was a brave man who denounced the slavery of his day. Legend has it that he never died and that he will return some day to announce the coming of a new world in which war, human cruelty, and the enslavement of one person by another will find no place. In his image, he embodies the vision of all wise people, his spirit brings a message of hope for the future, brings faith in the goodness of humanity, and brings the assurance that freedom will come to all.

Let us open the door and invite Elijah to enter and join with us as we drink the wine of our freedom.

***Everyone:*** *Fill the fourth cup of wine; open door and all rise. All say:*

May the spirit of Elijah enter the hearts of all of us, and inspire us to build a good world, in which justice and freedom shall be the inheritance of all people.

***Everyone:*** *Raise glasses and say:*

We raise the last cup of wine and affirm our unity with all people in the struggles for human freedom.

May slavery give way to freedom.
May hate give way to love.
May ignorance give way to wisdom.
May despair give way to hope.
Next year, at this time, may everyone, everywhere, be free!

***Everyone:*** *Put wine back down.*

### Who was Elijah?

Elijah was a biblical prophet who lived in the 9th century BCE in Israel. He was a fierce defender of God in the face of pagan influences, and he was given the honour of being named the "guardian angel" of the Jewish people. Because he did such a great job of defending God (especially compared to the other prophets), he was said to be the forerunner of the Messiah. In the Book of Malachi (the final book in the Old Testament), Malachi, who was the last of the Hebrew prophets, states that Elijah will reappear just before the coming of the Messianic Age.

### Why do we give Elijah his own cup of wine at Passover?

askmoses.com says: "On the night when we celebrate our redemption from Egypt, we also express our absolute belief in the coming of the Messiah, the one who will lead us out of this exile and take us all back to our land. We are so confident of our imminent redemption, that we actually pour a cup for Elijah, the prophet who will come to announce the arrival of the Messiah."

There is another reason for giving Elijah his own cup, though, and it's related to how many cups of wine we drink at Passover. You see, the four cups of wine that we drink during the meal relates to the four expressions of redemption (spoken by God to Moses) in the Book of Exodus:

"I am the Lord, and **I will bring you out** from under the burdens of the Egyptians, and **I will deliver you** from their bondage, and **I will redeem**

**you** with an out-stretched arm and with great acts of judgment, and **I will take you** for my people, and I will be your God; and you shall know that I am the Lord your God, who has brought you out from under the burdens of the Egyptians."

The next verse, "And **I will bring you** into the land which I swore to give to Abraham, to Isaac, and to Jacob; I will give it to you for a possession. I am the Lord" was not fulfilled until the generation following the Passover story, and the rabbis could not decide whether this verse counted as part of the Passover celebration (thus deserving of another serving of wine). So a compromise was made: a cup is left for the arrival of Elijah, but we don't drink it.

Other reasons are also given for why we drink four cups of wine. Some say the cups represent our matriarchs – Sarah, Rebecca, Rachel and Leah – whose virtue caused God to liberate us from slavery. Another interpretation is that the cups represent the Kabbalists' four worlds (physicality, emotions, thought and essence). But these explanations don't help to explain the reason for the fifth cup – Elijah's cup.

### What about Miriam? I'm sure I've heard of "Miriam's Cup" too somewhere...

Some households do indeed have "Miriam's Cup" too. Miriam was Moses's sister (see Chapter 6e: Maggid). She was considered a prophetess because she predicted that Moses would lead the Israelites to freedom. She was so certain of her brother's abilities that she brought her tambourine with her during the Exodus from Egypt, so that she could lead the women in singing and dancing. Surprisingly, there are no records of this ever getting on people's nerves: everyone seemed to enjoy the optimism.

*Miriam's Cup is traditionally filled with water, and it represents the miraculous well that accompanied the Israelites on their journey in the desert, providing them with water. The well was given by God to Miriam, to honour her bravery and devotion.*

*Miriam's Cup is a fairly recent Passover tradition, aimed at evening out the patriarchal bias associated with traditional Passover services. Indeed, having a feminist "edge" to Passover makes perfect sense: women, after all, had to step outside their familiar roles in society while wandering the desert on their Exodus from Egypt.*

*Many households say a blessing over Miriam's Cup too. There is no set blessing (and indeed no set part of the service in which to say the blessing), but you could say the following: "This is the cup of Miriam, a cup of living water and a reminder of the Exodus from Egypt. It symbolises loving, kindness, hope and renewal in our lives today."*

# 17 HALLEL (SONGS OF PRAISE) AND NIRTZAH (COMPLETE THE SEDER)

## Hallel

*You can find Hallel in all good Haggadahs. Warning: they're quite long.*

*OR...*

**Everyone:** *Or just say the prayer over the fourth cup of wine:*

בָּרוּךְ אַתָּה יְהֹוָה, אֱלֹהֵינוּ מֶלֶךְ הָעוֹלָם בּוֹרֵא פְּרִי הַגָּפֶן:

Baruch attah Adonai, eloheynu melech ha-olam, boray p'ri ha-gafen.

Blessed are You, Lord, our God, King of the universe, who creates the fruit of the vine.

**Everyone:** *Drink the fourth cup of wine, close the door and be seated.*

### What is Hallel?

*Hallel is a Jewish prayer – a verbatim recitation from Psalms 113–118 – which is used for praise and thanksgiving on Jewish holidays. There are two versions: full Hallel and partial Hallel.*

*Not everyone recites the Hallel at Passover – it's usually only done by the most observant of Jews. So, you know, if it's late and you're tired and you've got to make the kids' matzah sandwiches for school in the morning...it's not the end of the world if you don't do this bit.*

### What are the Psalms referred to above?

*Psalms is a book of the Hebrew Bible. Taken together, its 150 sacred poems express the full range of Israel's faith.*

## Nirtzah

*Everyone:* *Say:*

Next year in Jerusalem!

# REFERENCES

The following sources were used in the creation of this Haggadah:

- "Allexperts.com." AllExperts. Web. <http://allexperts.com>.

- Askmoses.com - Torah, Judaism and Jewish Info - Ask the Rabbi. Web. <http://www.askmoses.com>.

- Atkin, Yekutiel. "The Pesach Haggadah - and My Journey through It." The Jewish Magazine. Web. <http://www.jewishmag.com/122mag/passover-haggadah/haggadah.pdf>.

- Chabad.org. Web. <http://www.chabad.org>.

- Elwell, Ellen Sue Levi. Open Door ; a Passover Haggadah. New York: Central Conference of American Rabbis, 2002. Print.

- Encyclopædia Britannica. Web. <http://www.britannica.com>.

- Goodman, Jill. "Our Passover Haggadah." Happy Hippie. Web. <http://www.happyhippie.net/>.

- "The History of Passover." Sichos In English. Web. <http://www.sichosinenglish.org/cgi-bin/calendar?holiday=pesach>.

- "Home Rituals for Erev Rosh Hashanah." Scheinerman.net. Web. <http://scheinerman.net/judaism/hhd/rh-home.html>.

- Kaiserman, Saul. "Teaching Birkat Ha-Mazon: The Grace After Meals." Lookstein.org. Web. <http://www.lookstein.org/resources/birkat_hamazon.pdf>.

- Leman, Derek. "Understanding the Passover Haggadah, Part 3 | Messianic Jewish Musings." Messianic Jewish Musings | Messianic Jewish Theology and Biblical Reflection. Comments: Derek4messiah@gmail.com. Web. <http://derek4messiah.wordpress.com/2009/03/16/understanding-the-passover-haggadah-part-3>.

- The Open Source Haggadah. Web. <http://www.opensourcehaggadah.com/>.

- "The Passover Haggadah – a Guide to the Seder." The Jewish Federations of North America. Web. <http://www.jewishfederations.org/local_includes/downloads/39497.pdf>.

- "Passover Primer - 15 Steps of the Seder." Jewish Federation of Greater Atlanta. Web. <http://www.jewishatlanta.org/page.aspx?id=36809>.

- Rabbi Amy Scheinerman. "Passover Haggadah." Scheinerman.net/. Web. <http://scheinerman.net/>.

- Rabbi Jonathan Klein. "Birkat Hamazon." Hillel - The Foundation for Jewish Campus Life. Web. <www.hillel.org/NR/rdonlyres/222A6F13-ABF3-4704-B297-58E1244D FA1F/0/BirkatHamazon.pdf>.

- Rabbi Mosher Ben Asher PhD, and Magidah Khulda Bat Sarah. "Birkat Hamazon to Arouse Our Spirit." Gather The People. Web. <www.gatherthepeople.org>.

- Rabbi Rachel Barenblat. "Haggadah for Passover." Haggadah for Passover. Web. <http://velveteenrabbi.com/2006-Haggadah.pdf>.

- Rubiner, Michael. "The Two-minute Haggadah." Slate Magazine - Politics, Business, Technology, and the Arts - Slate Magazine. Web. <http://www.slate.com/id/2139601>.

- Soffer, Matt D. "An Analysis of Birkat HaMazon in Birkon Mikdash M'at: NFTY's Bencher." Matt Soffer. Web. <http://www.mattsoffer.com>.

- "The Thirty Minute Seder." Oceanside Jewish Center. Web. <www.oceansidejc.org/Haggadah/30-Minute-Seder_5765.pdf>.

- "The Union Haggadah: The Seder Service: The Story of the Oppression." Internet Sacred Text Archive. Web. <http://www.sacred-texts.com/jud/uh/uh12.htm>.

- Wagner, Jordan L. "The Transliterated Siddur." The Transliterated Siddur. Siddur.org. Web. <http://siddur.org/>.

- Wikipedia. Web. <http://wikipedia.org>.

- "Yeshuat Yisrael Passover Haggadah Messianic Jewish Synagogue." Congregation Yeshuat Yisrael. Web. <http://www.yeshuatyisrael.com/PDF/Passover%20Haggadah%20shor t.pdf>.

# HAGGADAH GOOD FEELING ABOUT THIS

Made in United States
Orlando, FL
21 April 2024

46025562R00040